The Disenfranchisement of the Negro

John L. Love

ISBN-13: 978-1523442331
ISBN-10: 1523442336

Table of Contents

I

"A Constitution formed so as to enable a party to overrule its very government, and to overpower the people too, answers the purpose neither of government nor of freedom"—Edmund Burke.

The assault, under the forms of law, which is being made upon the political rights of the Negro is the symptom of an animus which has its roots imbedded in the past. It does not mark a revival, but rather the supreme desperate effort of the spirit of tyranny to compass the political subjection and consequent social degradation of the black man. Its provocation does not consist in any abnormal or perilous condition in southern communities arising from a numerical preponderance of Negroes. It is not made to meet a merely temporary emergency with the intent to return to the principles of republican government upon the advent of intelligence and wealth to the Negro. Indeed, the very intent and purpose of the assault is to prevent such an advent, in so far as human ingenuity and tyrannical violence can do so.

It can not find its justification in a necessity of averting by radical measures any imagined perils to social order which might arise from the political domination of ignorance; for the spirit which prompts the assault has ever fostered ignorance and endeavored to perpetuate it. In fact, the assault is so iniquitous in its conception and is being executed with such wicked and violent disregard of political morals and human rights, as by comparison to render almost beneficent the realization of the perils which the imagination of the assailants pretends to fancy.

There may be those who see in this assault nothing more than a supreme effort of a benign civilization to save itself from utter ruin. It is, however, to be borne in mind that the apostles of this civilization which is of a peculiarly local type, have ever asserted that its maintenance and future glory are inseparably connected with the subjection of the Negro. Always they have spoken the language of tyranny, which, in spite of its embellishments and jugglings, amounts to this: the social well-being and political privileges of the Negro are inconsistent with the economic interests and political ambitions of a few southern white men. Into this language all of the feigned social[Pg 4] perils and political nightmares of southern planters and politicians easily resolve themselves.

There may be those who indulge the hope that the final triumph of this assault will have a salutary effect upon the social status of the Negro. Their hope is due in no small measure to their ignorance of the history of the character, spirit, and dominant purpose of the assailants. That history furnishes the best key to an understanding of the present assault upon the political rights of the Negro.

Forty years ago the slave power plunged this nation into war for the avowed purpose of perpetuating Negro slavery. Alexander Stevens, on his return from the convention which had erected the Southern Confederacy, addressing a large assembly at Savannah, uttered the following significant words:

"The new Constitution has put at rest forever all the agitating questions relating to our peculiar institution—African slavery as it exists among us—the proper status of the Negro in our form of civilization. This was the immediate cause of the late rupture and the present revolution."

Referring to the ideas of Thomas Jefferson and the leading statesmen at the time of the formation of the Federal Constitution, that Negro Slavery was in violation of the laws of Nature, wrong in "principle, socially, morally and politically," he continued thus:

"Those ideas were fundamentally wrong. They rested upon the assumption of the equality of races. Our constitution (the Confederate Constitution,) is founded upon exactly the opposite ideas. Its foundations are laid, its corner stone rests upon the great truth that the Negro is not equal to the white man; that slavery, subordination to the superior race, is his natural and normal condition."

It has become the rule to frown upon any and all references to the circumstances and causes that produced the Civil War. This is true especially of the men and women who upheld the cause of the

Union as against Secession. Naturally magnanimous, they have been at great pains to avoid in their public utterances any references to the "late unpleasantness" which might in any way wound the sensibilities of the excessively sensitive South. Certainly, nothing can be more sincerely desired than the utter eradication of the passions and animosities that were evoked by armed conflict. But to ignore the fundamental cause and motive which led the South to precipitate the war, with a view to seeming not to be influenced by sectional prejudices is pushing magnanimity to the verge of vapid sentimentality—a folly in which the South, in so far as its attitude toward the Negro is concerned, has in no sense shared.

The doctrine of "the proper status of the Negro," is as consistently maintained by the South in eighteen hundred and ninety-nine as in eighteen hundred and sixty, when it was made the shibboleth of the Slavery Party and the tocsin of war; and there can be no proper consideration of our present Negro Problem without regard to this historical doctrine.

The Southern Confederacy is now a political myth. In its attempt to make Negro Slavery its corner stone, it carved the gravestones of more than a million men. Upon the proclamation of peace and universal freedom, the nation's joy was without bounds. In the intense enthusiasm of the moment over the "new birth of freedom," and the overthrow of the slave power, the doctrine of the "proper status of the Negro" seemed to be eternally repudiated and the agitations relating to it seemed indeed "forever settled." But in the throes of its joy, there suddenly dawned upon the nation the fact that the problems pertaining to the Negro had, because of freedom, become more stupendous than even the question of slavery had been. Henceforth the Negro Problem was to test severely the integrity of republican principles.

This was the critical period of the history of the Negro in America. Within almost the twinkling of an eye, by an exigency of one of the world's greatest wars, his status had been suddenly changed. The slave became a free man by the dispensation of Providence and against the will of his master.

A free man, yet penniless and homeless. A man of toil, but one whose own and whose ancestral toil had created a material and social grandeur which now mocked at his poverty and arrogantly denied him a share in its blessings. A free man, but ignorant, the greatest curse imposed by his former status which had contributed to the enlightenment of others. A freeman, but helpless in the face of an impending persecution. He, whose labor had contributed to the comfort and social happiness of others,—who, while they were testing on scores of battle fields their power to rob him of his freedom, was caring for and protecting their wives and daughters and furnishing the sinews of the unholy war—was now at the mercy of those who had gone forth to battle with the cry that, "slavery, subordination to the superior race, is his natural and normal condition."

The Thirteenth Amendment became the law of the land through the travail of war. But the war had sapped the Nation's strength, had cost nearly a million lives and created a debt of three billions. Weary of strife and vexation, the nation was fain to leave the settlement of the problems, to which the new status of the Negro had given rise, to those among whom he was to live, i.e., to his former masters.

This was indeed a critical period in the history of the Negro race in the United States and the lessons of this period are exceedingly important in the light of the present attack upon the political rights of the black man.

In recent discussions of the merits and wisdom of Negro suffrage, this period is as a rule strangely overlooked. The assertion so commonly made, that the conferring of the right to vote upon the Negro was a colossal blunder, evinces the extent to which this period has been ignored by those who make it, or else their remarkable ignorance of the history of Negro suffrage. Political prejudices and the blind zeal and opportunism of those who have discovered some "sure cure," for the Negro's ills have aided much in the work of discrediting Negro suffrage. Some have ignored the facts to such an extent as to assert that Negro suffrage was the result of vindictiveness on the part of the

Northerners, who wished both to humiliate the South and to perpetuate the power of the Republican Party. The trouble with this assertion is that it imputes too much to Northern sagacity. What the nation, through the agency of the Republican party, did was to enact the Thirteenth Amendment and thus to make President Lincoln's conditional proclamation of freedom an unconditioned part of the organic law. The extent of its revenge was to insist upon the incorporation of this principle of freedom into the old Slave Constitutions of the South. This was the terms of surrender and having accepted this, the South was left alone (the boon it has always craved) with full power to deal with the Negro as tenderly as it saw fit. The Negro was left a "sojourner on sufferance" in the great republic which he had assisted in saving, and to the sweet charity of those who had sought to destroy it for the purpose of binding him with unbreakable chains.

By the acceptance of the terms imposed, the rebellious states placed themselves in a position of great responsibility and great opportunity. The responsibility of the old South, the South of slavery and rebellion, was to properly adjust itself to the new conditions of freedom and inseparable union, its opportunity was to prove to the nation the claim it so often and so boastfully makes that it is the Negro's best friend and is disposed to treat him fairly.

Did the South rise to its opportunity? Did it treat liberally and kindly those freedmen who as slaves had created its material wealth and many of whom as soldiers had with the irony of fate helped to keep it from separating from the Union of which it is now proud of being an integral part? Did it hold out to them the promise of gradual citizenship, and, in order that this citizenship should be intelligent, establish schools for their education? Was it jealous or in any way solicitous about the economic and industrial freedom of these people? In its bearing upon the present disfranchising enactments of the South, the answer to these questions is important.

Unaccustomed to free schools, trained to despise and punish the intellectual aspirations of the slave, these recently rebellious states not only refused to educate the freedmen, but actually burned many schools that were built by men and women of the North, who in obedience to genuine Christian charity followed in the wake of the armies of freedom. Then as now, it proceeded to fix the Negro's status by hostile legislation in the shape of Black codes. These laws reveal the deliberate purpose of the South to reduce the freedmen to a state of serfdom more bitter and degrading than slavery had been, and violated the most sacred of the inherent rights of human nature.

The civilized state of Alabama, which is now preparing to disfranchise the Negro, declared that "stubborn and refractory servants, and servants who loiter away their time," were to be treated as vagrants, fined fifty dollars and "in default of payment might be hired out at public auction for a period of six months." Thus the Thirteenth Amendment did not destroy the auction block.

Florida declared that "it shall not be lawful for any Negro or person of color to own, use, or keep any bowie knife, dirk, sword or fire arms or ammunition of any kind" without license, to be granted only upon the recommendation of two "respectable" white men. For violating this law the Negro was to stand in the pillory for one hour and then be whipped with thirty-nine lashes on the bare back. South Carolina, always bold to reveal its purpose, declared that "no person of color shall pursue the practice, art, trade or business of an artisan, mechanic, shopkeeper or any other employment besides that of husbandry or that of a servant under contract for labor" without a license, which was good for one year only; and she supplemented this with the following:

"That a person of color, who is in the employment of a master engaged in husbandry, shall not have the license to sell any corn, rice, peas, wheat or other grain, any flour, cotton, fodder, hay, bacon, fresh meat of any kind or any other product of a farm, without written permission of such master."

Louisiana, which has recently outlawed the Negro by Constitutional enactment, declared:

"Every adult freedman or woman shall furnish themselves with a comfortable home and visible means of support within twenty days after the passage of this act!"

Failing to do so, such persons were to be hired out at public auction for the rest of the year.

Let it be borne in mind that these laws were not enactments of a distant and forgotten past. They were the deliberate enactments of that period for the purpose of nullifying the Thirteenth Amendment.

Of this period Mr. Justice Miller in rendering the decision in the Slaughter House Cases said:

"The process of restoring to their proper relations with the Federal Government and with the other states those which had sided with the rebellion, undertaken under the proclamation of President Johnson in 1865, and before the assembling of Congress, developed the fact that, notwithstanding the formal recognition by those states of the abolition of slavery, the condition of the slave race would, without further protection of the Federal Government, be almost as bad as it was before. Among the first acts of legislation adopted by several of the states in the legislative bodies which claimed to be in their normal relations with the Federal Government, were laws which imposed upon the colored race onerous disabilities and burdens, and curtailed their rights in the pursuit of life, liberty, and property to such an extent that their freedom was of little value, while they had lost their protection which they had received from their former owners from motives both of interest and humanity."

This is what happened to the Negro when the South was left alone to deal with him and when he was voteless.

James G. Blaine truly said that:

"Without the right of citizenship his freedom could be maintained only in name, and without the elective franchise his citizenship would have no legitimate and no authoritative protection."

Fortunately for the Negro and for the continuance of free institutions in the South, the nation slowly perceived this truth, but not until a long and bitter struggle had been carried on by the friends of freedom for manhood suffrage and human rights. These infamous, repressive and enslaving laws finally aroused the nation's sense of justice and brought it to the realization of the undeniable truth that in a free government "the strong keen sword by which a freeman can protect all other rights and give value to all other privileges is the elective franchise."

Yet in the full consciousness of this truth, attested beyond cavil by the inhuman subjection of the Negro to the arrogant and oppressive will of those who held peculiar notions about his "proper status," the Federal Government hesitated to go the full length of its duty. It stopped midway. The war seemed not to have convinced it of the futility and fatality of compromising with the South. The

Fourteenth Amendment was adopted. The Negro was thereby given the right which his Southern guardians proudly refused him—the right of citizenship—but not the right which is alone the guarantee of the privileges of citizenship—the right to a voice in the government of which he was declared a citizen. The power of conferring suffrage limited or universal, was left as the special privilege of the South. But the South proceeded to nullify the Fourteenth Amendment as it had nullified the Thirteenth and sent her captains of rebellion to make the nation's laws.

Impelled by the motive of self preservation, by the sheer necessity of saving itself from those who would have destroyed it, and of saving to the freedmen the simple inherent right of self-ownership, the nation was forced to confer upon the Negro the right to vote by the adoption of the Fifteenth Amendment. This step it is now popular to characterize as a blunder or as an act of revenge designed to humiliate the South. If it was, then the preservation of the Union and the abolition of slavery are nameless crimes.

The period of Reconstruction has served as the text for discrediting Negro Suffrage and is always the apt illustration that gives point to the argument of those who attempt to prove the incapacity of the Negro to exercise the right of suffrage. There is no doubt that the effort to mould public sentiment away from Negro Suffrage has been generally successful and this success has been achieved very largely through misrepresentation in regard to the facts of Reconstruction. The great body of active citizens have grown into full citizenship since the Reconstruction epoch, are consequently ignorant of its true history and quite satisfied to receive the information concerning it from those whose interest and delight it is to resort to misrepresentation.

It is not my purpose to enter into a defense of Reconstruction, but merely to call attention to the following facts:

(1) The attempt to reconstruct the rebellious states along lines of Republican principles failed until the Negro was given the right to vote. Those who had participated in the War of the Rebellion and to whom the opportunity had been given to return to normal relations with the Federal Government without the interference of the Negro, failed signally and deliberately to do so in an acceptable manner. Negro Suffrage was therefore an essential and beneficent factor in the work of reconstruction.

(2) The accepted history of that period has been written by those who rode into power by murder and intimidation and to whose interest it is to paint the history of reconstruction so dark as to hide their own flagrant crimes. Their method of history writing has been that of suppression and distortion of facts.

(3) The true history of that period reveals some things that place Negro Suffrage in a remarkably creditable light.

The statement has recently been made that "the reconstruction regime in the South worked lasting injury to the colored race."Place this statement in juxtaposition with a few of the things that were really done by these newly enfranchised people who were practicing their first lessons in the science of government.

Judge Albion W. Tourgee has stated it thus:

"They obeyed the Constitution of the United States, and annulled the bonds of states, counties, and cities which had been issued to carry on the war of rebellion and maintain armies in the field against the Union. They instituted a public school system in a realm where public schools had been unknown. They opened the ballot box and jury box to thousands of white men who had been debarred from them by a lack of earthly possessions. They introduced home rule into the South. They abolished the whipping post, the branding iron, the stocks and other barbarous forms of punishment which had up to that time prevailed. They reduced capital felonies from about twenty to two or three. In an age of extravagance they were extravagant in the sums appropriated for public works. In all of that time no man's rights of person were invaded under the forms of law. Every Democrat's life, home, fireside and business were safe. No man obstructed any white man's way to the ballot box, interfered with his freedom of speech or boycotted him on account of his political faith."

This is the record which it is said "has worked lasting injury to the colored race." If the true history of this period proves anything it is this, namely, that the only republican government in fact as well as in form that has ever existed in the South was when the Negro, though a mere tyro in the art of government, was a controlling factor in southern politics. His "lasting injury" consists in the fact that he planted "the seeds of all the New South's prosperity."

The Southern politicians, who in their desperation to perpetuate Negro Slavery created a national debt of more than three billions and stained every vale and hillside with the blood of freemen, point with ineffable horror at the extravagant financial legislation of the Reconstruction period. It may be that this much paraded extravagance amounts to more than the fiction of distorted facts; but, in view of the audacious corruption of the era which preceded it, and the gigantic peculations of that which has followed, the financial profligacy of Reconstruction may not have been so bad after all.

Replying to a characteristic speech of Senator Tillman delivered in the recent South Carolina Constitutional Convention, in which he arraigned the financial legislation of Reconstruction in that State Mr. Thomas E. Miller, one of the six Negro members of the convention, said:

"The gentleman from Edgefield (Mr. Tillman) speaks of the piling up of the State debt; of jobbery and peculation during the period between 1869 and 1873 in South Carolina, but he has not found voice eloquent enough, nor pen exact enough to mention those imperishable gifts bestowed upon South Carolina between 1873 and 1876 by Negro legislators—the laws relative to finance, the building of penal and charitable institutions, and, greatest of all, the establishment of the public school system. Starting as infants in legislation in 1869, many wise measures were not thought of, many injudicious acts were passed. But in the administration of affairs for the next four years, having learned by experience the result of bad acts, we immediately passed reformatory laws touching every department of state, county, municipal and town governments. These enactments are today upon the statute books of South Carolina. They stand as living witnesses of the Negro's fitness to vote and legislate upon the rights of mankind.

"When we came into power town governments could lend the credit of their respective towns to secure funds at any rate of interest that the council saw fit to pay. Some of the towns paid as high as 20 per cent. We passed an act prohibiting town governments from pledging the credit of their hamlets for money bearing a greater rate of interest than 5 per cent.

"Up to 1874, inclusive, the State Treasurer had the power to pay out State funds as he pleased. He could elect whether he would pay out the funds on appropriations that would place the money in the hands of the peculators, or would apply them to appropriations that were honest and necessary. We saw the evil of this and passed an act making specific levies and collections of taxes for specific appropriations.

"Another source of profligacy in the expenditure of funds was the law that provided for and empowered the levying and collecting of special taxes by school districts, in the name of the schools. We saw its evil and by a constitutional amendment provided that there should only be levied and collected annually a tax of two mills for school purposes, and took away from the school districts the power to levy and to collect taxes of any kind. By this act we cured the evils that had been inflicted upon us in the name of the schools, settled the public school question for all time to come, and established the system upon an honest, financial basis.

"Next, we learned during the period from 1869 to 1874, inclusive, that what was denominated the floating indebtedness, covering the printing schemes and other indefinite expenses amounted to nearly $2,000,000. A conference was called of the leading Negro representatives in the two houses together with the State Treasurer, also a Negro. After this conference we passed an act for the purpose of ascertaining the bona fide floating debt and found that it did not amount to more than

$250,000 for the four years; we created a commission to sift that indebtedness and to scale it. Hence when the Democratic party came into power they found the floating debt covering the legislative and all other expenditures, fixed at the certain sum of $250,000. This same class of Negro legislators led by the State Treasurer, Mr. F. L. Cardoza, knowing that there were millions of fraudulent bonds charged against the credit of the state, passed another act to ascertain the true bonded indebtedness, and to provide for its settlement. Under this law, at one sweep, those entrusted with the power to do so, through Negro legislators, stamped six millions of bonds, denominated as conversion bonds, "fraudulent." The commission did not finish its work before 1876. In that year, when the Hampton government came into power, there were still to be examined into and settled under the terms of the act passed by us providing for the legitimate bonded indebtedness of the state, a little over two and a half million dollars worth of bonds and coupons which had not been passed upon.

"Governor Hampton, General Hagood, Judge Simonton, Judge Wallace and in fact, all of the conservative thinking Democrats aligned themselves under the provision enacted by us for the certain and final settlement of the bonded indebtedness and appealed to their Democratic legislators to stand by the Republican legislation on the subject and to confirm it. A faction in the

Democratic party obtained a majority of the Democrats in the legislature against settling the question and they endeavored to open up anew the whole subject of the state debt. We had a little over thirty members in the house and enough Republican senators to sustain the Hampton conservative faction and to stand up for honest finance, or by our votes place the debt question of the old state into the hands of the plunderers and peculators. We were appealed to by General Hagood, through me, and my answer to him was in these words: 'General, our people have learned the difference between profligate and honest legislation. We have passed acts of financial reform, and with the assistance of God when the vote shall have been taken, you will be able to record for the thirty odd Negroes, slandered though they have been through the press, that they voted solidly with you all for honest legislation and the preservation of the credit of the state.' The thirty odd Negroes in the legislature and their senators, by their votes did settle the debt question and saved the state $13,000,000. We were eight years in power. We had built school houses, established charitable institutions, built and maintained the penitentiary system, provided for the education of the deaf and dumb, rebuilt the jails and court houses, rebuilt the bridges and re-established the ferries. In short, we had reconstructed the state and placed it upon the road to prosperity and, at the same time, by our acts of financial reform transmitted to the Hampton Government an indebtedness not greater by more than $2,500,000 than was the bonded debt of the State in 1868, before the Republican Negroes and their white allies came into power."

With the disgraceful dicker of 1877, this era closed, and with it passed away for a time, whose limit has not yet been fixed, whatever there has been, of republican government in the South. How the overthrow of Reconstruction government was accomplished is well-known. The significance of its overthrow is that it marked the arrogant reassertion of the malignant and desperate purpose of the southern oligarchy, trained in the absolutism of slave mastery, to despoil the Negro of the rights of citizenship, and to reduce him to a state of serfdom.

In the preparation for the execution of this infamous purpose, they attempted and succeeded in accomplishing what does great credit to the sheer audacity of southern political leadership. By sublime dissimulation they hoodwinked the other sections of the country in regard to the South's attitude to the Negro. Their first maneuver was to give the Negro a bad reputation and denounce as mischievous meddlers those who insisted that he be dealt with justly. The Southern oligarchy put forward its youngest and best men. Its first point of attack was Massachusetts; and thither went Grady and Gordon and Watterson who with persuasive accent plead the cause of the "New South." With charming recklessness of statement, they proclaimed the era of sectional fraternity and with consummate cunning set forth in the next breath to eastern capitalists the industrial possibilities of the South. Gradually they reached the climax of their mission, to wit: Leave the Negro to us: we are his friends, his natural guardians: we know him better than you do, and can more wisely fix his status in our social scheme. Then the old, old story was repeated with endless refrain, of the Negro's ignorance, criminal tendencies (fully attested by timely news dispatches from the South), of his inferiority, and of the menace he is to Anglo-Saxon domination.

Thus while the sons of slave masters were poisoning the minds of the north and west, the slave drivers were at home perfecting the conspiracy against Negro citizenship.

The year 1890 witnessed the beginning of the execution of this conspiracy which promises to continue until the Negro is divested of every right which is worth the having. In 1890 a minority of the people of the state of Mississippi arrogated to themselves the right to despoil the majority of the citizens of that state of the rights of free men by nullifying the Fifteenth Amendment.

II

Before considering the new constitutions of the States of Mississippi, South Carolina and Louisiana, and the decisions of courts respecting them, I have deemed it proper to review the history of Negro Suffrage and to indicate the unvarying attitude of the ruling classes of the South towards it. In the light of this history, let us now briefly examine these recent enactments in their relation to the political rights of the Negro.

It is no secret that the avowed purpose of the framers of these instruments was to deprive the Negro of the right to vote. Their purpose is not more startling than is the defiance with which they have hurled it from the housetops. This purpose they claim to have accomplished by taking advantage of the ignorance and poverty of the Negro; but the most cursory glance at these enactments will convince any one that neither intelligence nor wealth constitutes the basis of electoral qualification under them, while the confessions of the framers of them as well as their operation proves that neither ignorance nor poverty serves to disqualify.

In Mississippi a Negro may be as rich as Dives and as wise as Solomon and yet he may not be able to satisfy an ignorant and partisan registration officer that he is qualified to be an elector; while a white man may be as poor as Lazarus and may not possess the intellectual outfit of a Hottentot and yet he will experience no difficulty in convincing the same individual that he is qualified to exercise all the rights and privileges of that class whose "destiny it is to dominate." This is the sort of educational qualifications these great constitutional documents prescribe!

How to disfranchise the Negro by an educational test without at the same time disfranchising a very large number of white men, was at first a problem that presented many difficulties to the framers of the Mississippi document. Such a problem, however, cannot long remain a difficult one to men who are masters of the art of legalizing fraud.

That the illiterate white vote might not, by the play of accident, become eliminated by an educational test, it was provided that that part of the constitution which prescribes it, was not to go into operation until one year after the adoption of the constitution. Before the expiration of that time another standard of qualification was provided and all who qualified under it were not to be affected by the subsequent operation of the educational test.

This latter provision is as follows, being section 241 of Article 12 of the constitution of Mississippi, defining who are electors:

"Every male inhabitant of the state, except idiots, insane persons, and Indians not taxed, who is a citizen of the United States, twenty-one years of age and upwards, who has resided in the state two years, and one year in the election district in which he offers to vote and who is duly registered as provided in this article, and who has never been convicted of bribery, burglary, theft, arson, obtaining money or goods under false pretense, perjury, embezzlement, or bigamy, and who has paid on or before the first day of February of the year in which he offers to vote, all taxes which may have been legally required of him and who shall produce to the officer holding the election satisfactory evidence that he has paid his taxes."

Under this section of the Mississippi constitution, the white population of that state qualified as electors. But to prevent the Negroes from qualifying, section 242 of Article 12, further provides that persons offering to register shall take the following oath:

"I do solemnly swear that I am twenty one years old and that I will have resided in the state two years and (this) election district for one year preceding the ensuing election, and am now in good faith a resident of the same, and that I am not disqualified from voting by reason of having been convicted of any of the crimes mentioned in the constitution of this state as a disqualification to be an elector, that I will truly answer all questions propounded to me concerning my antecedents so far as they relate to my right to vote and also as to my residence before my citizenship in this district, that I will support the constitution of the United States and of the state of Mississippi and will bear true faith and allegiance to the same - so help me God.

Any willful and corrupt false statement in said affidavit or in answer to any material question propounded as herein authorized shall be perjury."

In the foregoing provisions attention is called to the following:

(1) The crimes mentioned as disqualifying from voting are such as it is always easy, when desirable, to convict the Negro of committing. Under the present method of administering justice in the states where these disfranchising constitutions operate, the Negro has neither any guarantee of a fair and impartial trial nor any protection against malicious prosecution or false accusations when it is convenient to convict him.

(2) The penalty for not paying taxes almost a year before election day is a disqualification from voting. But this of course is not the sole penalty. Whether he is a qualified elector or not, every man must in the case of real property pay his taxes, or suffer the loss of his property, and certainly no man, not even the poorest of the Negroes and poor whites, can escape the obligation of the poll tax by a mere forfeiture of his right to vote. Thus the penalty for not paying taxes is twofold in so far as the Negro is concerned. The poor white man may or may not experience any difficulty about producing "to the officer holding the election satisfactory evidence that he has paid his taxes."

(3) The Negro who may desire to vote must answer under oath not certain specific interrogatories concerning his antecedents and

former places of residence, but to "truly answer all questions propounded" to him, with the understanding that the slightest mistake will be construed as a corrupt and willful false statement exposing him to prosecution for perjury, thus rendering him everlastingly disqualified to vote.

When, under the foregoing provision the white male inhabitants of the state became qualified electors, the following provision, being section 244 of article 12 of the constitution of Mississippi, went into operation:

"On and after the first day of January, 1892, every elector in addition to the foregoing qualifications, shall be able to read any section of the constitution of this state; or shall be able to understand the same when read to him, or give a reasonable interpretation thereof."

This section contains the so-called educational test, and the elector's qualifications under it are determined by a registration officer whose discretion is as limitless as his prejudices. The registration officers of South Carolina acting under a similar provision of the constitution of that state required the Negroes who offered themselves for registration to understand and explain section 4 of article 5 of the constitution of South Carolina, which is as follows:

"The supreme courts shall have power to issue writs or orders of injunctions, mandamus, quo warranto, prohibition, certiorari, habeas corpus, and other original and remedial writs, etc."

Fearing apparently that these provisions of the constitution might not prove a sufficient barrier to the Negro's intellect and cunning, the legislature of Mississippi has gone the full length of the power granted it, in its efforts to keep the Negro from voting. Section 3643 of the code of 1892 of that state, which regulates the appointment of managers of elections, contains this remarkably clever provision:

"The Commissions shall appoint three persons to be managers of election, who shall not be of the same political party, if suitable persons of different political parties can be had in the district."

Imagine commissioners of election of the Mississippi type regarding a Negro, or a white man known to be favorable to Negro suffrage, as a "suitable person!"

One would suppose that the elector having successfully passed the ordeal of the registration officer would be allowed smooth sailing during the remainder of the voyage to the polls. But no; having passed Scylla, he must encounter Charybdis at the very brink of the ballot box; for section 3644 of the above mentioned Code provides that any of the managers of election:

"May examine on oath any person duly registered and offering to vote touching his qualifications as an elector."

The effect of the constitution of Mississippi is to set up a standard of qualification of a much higher intellectual scale than that of any of the most enlightened states in the Union and to deprive a hundred and eighty thousand citizens of the elective franchise previously enjoyed by them.

The attempt is often made by southern politicians of the dominant class to justify the Mississippi plan of disfranchisement by pointing to the fact that Massachusetts, a northern state, has provided for a qualified suffrage by the adoption of an educational test. But compared with the Mississippi provision that of Massachusetts is as modest and simple as the average Mississippi school house.

Amendment XX to the Massachusetts Constitution is as follows:

"No person shall have the right to vote, or be eligible to office under the constitution of this commonwealth, who shall not be able to read the constitution in the English language, and write his name. Provided however, that the provisions of this amendment shall not apply to any person prevented by physical disability from complying with its requisition. Nor to any person, who now has the right to vote, nor to any person who shall be sixty years of age or upwards at the time this amendment shall take effect."

Thus Massachusetts requires that those wishing to exercise the elective franchise in the future must be able merely to read the English language; and expends annually more than four dollars per capita to educate them; while Mississippi requires, not only future electors, but those who have previously exercised the right to vote to give "a reasonable interpretation" to the satisfaction of a registration officer, and expends annually less than one dollar per capita for education!

Here it may be well to state that, although the idea of a qualified suffrage grew out of the desire and the necessity to prepare the foreign born element of our population, aliens to our institutions and language, for an intelligent exercise of the ballot, the Negro does not make objection or complaint to a just and fair educational test of his fitness to exercise the right of suffrage. Absolutely loyal to republical institutions, he is willing to go as far as any in the matter of fairly and justly protecting the ballot from abuses that grow out of ignorance.

The Constitution of Mississippi has served as the pattern for the disfranchising enactments of South Carolina and Louisiana. The main provision in the South Carolina Constitution regulating suffrage is as follows:

"Up to January 1, 1898, all male persons of voting age applying for registration, who can read any section of this constitution submitted to them, or understand and explain it when read to them by the registration officer, shall be entitled to registration and become electors."

It will be observed that the understanding and interpreting clause of the foregoing operates the reverse of that of the Constitution of Mississippi. The South Carolina provision was limited to cease after January 1, 1898, while that of Mississippi was limited to begin January 1, 1892 and to continue thereafter without ceasing.

Subdivision (d) of the above mentioned section of the South Carolina Constitution provides as follows:

"Any person who shall apply for registration after January 1, 1898, if otherwise qualified, shall be registered: Provided that he can both read and write any section of the constitution submitted to him by the registration officer or can show that he owns and has paid taxes collectible during the previous year on property in this state assessed at three hundred dollars ($300) or more."

Subdivision (c) of the South Carolina law effected the disfranchisement of more than one hundred thousand electors who had passed the legal age of attending school. But for this fact, the provision of subdivision (d) if fairly applied could meet with no objection. However, it cannot be absolutely fair as long as South Carolina expends less money per capita in the education of its Negro population than in the education of its white population. The report of the Superintendent of Education of South Carolina shows that it has cost $4.23 per capita to educate the white children of the state and only $1.35 per capita to educate the colored children.

When the present Constitution of South Carolina was in process of construction, the Supreme Court of the United States had not passed upon the legality of the so-called educational provision of the Mississippi Constitution, and the possibility that it might in the near future declare all such enactments repugnant to the Constitution of the United States deterred the members of the South Carolina constitutional convention from going the full length of the Mississippi plan. Although they had assembled for no other purpose than to disfranchise the Negro, yet out of fear of the Fifteenth Amendment to the Federal Constitution, they failed to do all they purposed.

George L. Tillman, the brother of the present United States Senator from that state, spoke in the convention the following significant and pathetic words:

"Mr. President, we can all hope a great deal from the constitution we have adopted. It is not such an instrument as we would have made had we been a free people. We are not a free people; we have not been since the war. I fear it will be some time before we can call ourselves free. I have had that fact very painfully impressed upon me for several years. If we were free, instead of having Negro suffrage we would have Negro slavery; instead of having the United States Government we would have the Confederate States Government; instead of paying $300,000 pension tribute we would be receiving it."

The Constitution of Louisiana, in its attempt to disfranchise the Negro and enfranchise, so to speak, every other class of men, the ignorant scum of Europe, as well as the intelligent and illiterate native born whites, outdoes both Mississippi and South Carolina. It adopts practically the same educational and property qualifications as are contained in the Mississippi and South Carolina instruments. The fifth section of it furnishes a true index to the spirit which is behind all of these disfranchising enactments. With vindictive memory, the framers of the Louisiana Constitution qualified as electors all who were entitled to vote on January 1, 1867 or at any date prior thereto as well as the sons and grandsons of such persons, whether or not they possess intelligence or property. Herein they display the same spirit which refused to accord to the Negro the right to vote previous to 1867.

What has been the attitude of the Courts towards these enactments which in the interest of oligarchy have set aside republican governments in the South and nullified the Constitution of the United States?

Naturally, the state courts have upheld them. The most remarkable judicial utterance since the famous Dred Scott decision is that of the supreme court of Mississippi in the case of Ratliff vs. Beale, predicated upon the constitution of Mississippi respecting the elective franchise. The Court said:

"Within the field of permissible action, under the limitations imposed by the Federal Constitution, the convention swept the circle of expedients to obstruct the exercise of the franchise by the Negro race. By reason of its previous condition of servitude and dependence, this race had acquired or accentuated certain peculiarities of habit, of temperament, and character, which clearly distinguished it as a race from that of the whites - a patient, docile people, careless, landless, and migratory within narrow limits, without forethought, and its criminal members given rather to furtive offenses than to the robust crimes of the whites. Restrained by the Federal Constitution from discriminating against the Negro race, the convention discriminated against its characteristics and the offenses to which its weaker members were prone."

Thus a court created by this new constitution of Mississippi declares that it, in spite of the Fifteenth Amendment, discriminates against the Negro race "by reason of its previous condition of servitude and dependence," and at the same time upholds that instrument.

"Though the law in itself be fair on its face and impartial in appearance, yet, if it be applied and administered by public authority with an evil eye and an unequal hand, so as to practically make unjust and illegal discriminations between persons in similar circumstances, material to their rights, the denial of equal justice is still within the prohibition of the Constitution."

There are other grounds for the belief that the Federal Supreme Court will refuse to sustain these instruments of disfranchisement, even though it has not of recent years acted in a manner to inspire faith.

These enactments have never received the approval of the people of the states. Of a total of 235,604 male citizens of voting age in South Carolina in 1890, more than 102,000 of whom were white men, only 60,925 participated in the election of November 6, 1894, at which the members of the constitutional convention were elected. Of the number thus voting only 31,402 were counted in favor of holding the convention. Thus one-seventh of the citizens called a convention and enacted a constitution which disfranchised more than one hundred thousand electors. The constitutions of Mississippi and Louisiana were adopted in the same way.

These so called constitutions, besides being repugnant to the spirit and purpose of the Fifteenth Amendment are also violative of the acts of Congress restoring the rebellious states to the Union, which acts [Pg 22]the Federal Supreme Court has on several occasions declared constitutional.

Pursuant to the reconstruction legislation, these states adopted constitutions admitting the Negro to the ballot and then asked to be readmitted to representation in Congress. Congress, having approved of their constitutions, enacted that they be entitled to representation in Congress, "upon the following fundamental conditions: That the constitutions of neither of said states shall ever be so amended or changed as to deprive any citizen or class of citizens of the United States of the right to vote in said states, who are entitled to vote by the constitution thereof herein recognized."

These states accepted these fundamental conditions and are consequently bound by them.

III

What effect have these disfranchising enactments had upon the status of the Negro? Has he lost nothing more than the bare right to vote? Has he been deprived of nothing but an abstract right to a voice in the affairs of government and of no other privilege than the possibility of a share of political power?

Surely the loss of any one of the foregoing is not unimportant in a democratic form of government. But he has lost much more, and the probabilities are that, if these obvious discriminations are allowed to continue, he will be brought to his deepest humiliation. The law which deprives him of the badge of citizenship, changes at once his legal status and cuts him off from respect. His disqualification as an elector shuts him out of the jury box in courts where what few rights he has left are adjudicated and his grievances redressed. His disqualification as an elector and as a juror discredits him as a witness. In the states which have adopted these disfranchising constitutions, more than three hundred thousand citizens have been thereby disqualified as jurors. This is all the more outrageous, because in the same states advantage has been taken in criminal legislation of what the Supreme Court of Mississippi has termed "certain peculiarities of habit and character of the Negro" whereby "furtive offenses," which in other communities are treated as mere misdemeanors, are made felonies and are usually visited with greater punishment than are the "robust crimes" of the whites. In South Carolina, for instance, the breach of a labor contract has been made a crime, the object being to reduce the Negro to a state of serfdom.

Not only has the legal status of the Negro been gravely affected by these disfranchising enactments; his economic status has also been lowered. A Mississippian states the following as the reason for disfranchising the Negro in his state:

"It is a question of political economy which the people of the North can not realize nor understand and which they have no right to discuss as they have no power to determine. If the Negro is permitted to engage in politics his usefulness as a laborer is at an end. He can no longer be controlled or utilized. The South has to deal with him as an industrial and economic factor and is forced to assert its control over him in sheer self-defense."

Thus Negro labor must be managed, and control must be asserted over him. His possession of the ballot would make him a free laborer and would enable him to demand the wages of free labor. It is truly an "economic problem," in which not only the Negro of the South is concerned, but also the interests of free labor in every section of this country.

These disfranchising enactments in that they lower the legal and economic status of the black man, also tend to lower his educational and social status. The political and economic supremacy of the southern oligarchy is dependent upon the ignorance and the social degradation of the Negro. It is, therefore, not surprising that the politicians now dominant in the South assert that education disqualifies him as a field hand,—as a manageable factor,—and that consequently there must be a decrease in the amount of money expended for his education or that his education must be directed along lines which will make him more adaptable to management as an economic factor for their sole benefit. The educated Negro is not more desirable now than he was fifty years ago. It is a marvel how the great body of southern white people, a great many of whom are favorable to the advancement of the Negro, will permit men of the type of the average politicians who now exercise control among them to stand thus in the way of the true progress of the South.

First, it is asserted that the right to vote destroys his usefulness as a laborer; then, that education turns his head and makes him discontented with the plantation where wages reach the high water mark of six dollars a month, which may or may not be paid according to the whim of his employer; and finally that the privilege of respectable accommodations furnished by common carriers which enjoy unusual public franchises makes him impudent, noisy and self-respecting, the proper remedy for which is a system of "Jim Crow Cars." Thus with the passing away of the Negro's right to vote, begins the reappearance of the odious system of Black Laws which are designed to degrade the womanhood and manhood of the Negro race. The whole trend of southern legislation is to fix what has been termed the "proper status of the Negro—subordination to the superior race." Not a single line has been written upon the statute books of a single southern state within the last decade in recognition of the Negro as a man entitled to respect, or fair and just consideration.

In 1857, Mr. Lincoln uttered the following words in reference to slavery, which are not wanting in significance in their bearing upon the present assault upon the Negro:

"To aid in making the bondage of the Negro universal and eternal, it (the Declaration of Independence) is assailed and sneered at, construed and hawked at and torn, till, if the framers could rise from their graves, they would hardly recognize it. All the powers of earth seem combined against him. Ambition follows, philosophy follows, and the theology of the day is fast joining in the cry. They have him in his prison house; they have searched his person and left no prying instrument with him; and now they have him as it were bolted with a lock of a hundred keys which can never be unlocked, except by the concurrence of every key in the hands of a hundred different men and they scattered to a hundred different places. And now they stand musing as to what invention in all the domain of mind and matter can be produced to make the impossibility of his escape more complete than it is."

The nation can not put up with many more of these instruments of disfranchisement. It can not endure the present ones very much longer. The question is ceasing to be one of interest merely to the Negro; it is rapidly becoming one of national moment. It is becoming a contest between democracy and oligarchy in which the stability and integrity of republican institutions are involved. Already a few thousand minions of oligarchy are exerting a larger influence in the national government than do millions of freemen who are obeying the Federal Constitution by maintaining a republican form of government. The election returns from the three states of Louisiana, South Carolina and Mississippi show how startling is the power which they exercise in Congress by reason of these disfranchising instruments. The following shows the number of votes polled in these states for members of Congress in 1898 and in the case of Louisiana the votes polled may be compared with the returns of 1896 when the old constitution was in force:

LOUISIANA

District.	Total Vote, 1898.	Total Vote, 1896.
I	6,318	15,412
II	7,856	16,848
III	5,903	15,968
IV	5,900	16,148
V	4,805	15,264
VI	2,494	16,482

| Average | 5,549 | Average | 16,020 |

MISSISSIPPI

SOUTH CAROLINA

District.	Total Vote, 1898.	District.	Total Vote, 1898.
I	2,468	I	4,559
II	3,175	II	4,138
III	2,661	III	4,361
IV	4,551	IV	4,632
V	5,105	V	4,230
VI	6,071	VI	4,916
VII	3,605	VII	4,938
Average	3,948	Average	4,539

The total congressional vote of Louisiana which elected six members to Congress is less by nearly 500 votes than the average for one district in Iowa. One elector in Louisiana exercises about seven times as much power in Congress as one in Ohio. The average congressional vote of Mississippi for seven districts is nearly 35,000 votes less than the average for twenty-one districts in Ohio, while the total congressional vote of South Carolina for seven Congressmen is more than seven thousand below the total vote of a single congressional district in North Carolina. The total vote cast in the twenty congressional districts of South Carolina, Louisiana, and Mississippi in the election of 1898 was 91,184; while that polled in the ten congressional districts of Wisconsin was

332,204. Thus, although these states cast nearly two hundred and fifty thousand votes less than the state of Wisconsin, they control twice as much power as that state in the national legislature.

The southern people themselves can not permit these violent infringements of the principles of republican government to continue without irrevocable detriment to their best and highest interests. In the degree that they stand by in silence and see the Negro stripped of his civil and political rights by a band of unscrupulous men who[Pg 26] seek no higher end than their personal aggrandizement, they compromise their own civil and political freedom, and put in jeopardy the industrial progress of the south. The bane of the South today is her selfish and misguided political leadership, the men who will not scruple to sacrifice upon the altars of their insatiable ambition for power every interest linked with her economic posperity and all consideration for civic virtue by which alone the greatness of a people is measured.

Her misfortune lies not in any danger from Negro domination, for of all the classes of her population the Negro is the least capable of working her injury and the least disposed to do so. Her real danger lies in the pernicious activity of her dominant political leaders who perpetuate their control by overriding local and national authority to the diminution of both public and private security. Law has been dethroned and the respectable and industrious portion of the people must witness the spectacle and endure the humiliation of riot, bloodshed, and assassination with impunity of innocent and unoffending citizens by the beneficiaries under these disfranchising constitutions.

The leading paper of the state of Louisiana, which threw the weight of its influence in favor of the constitutional convention which was held for the sole and avowed purpose of disfranchising the Negro, has recently made the following important confession:

"Assassination is still the order of the day and night in Tangipahoa Parish. William McGee, a white man, employed at a saw mill was the victim. He was waylaid yesterday morning and fired upon, with the result that he was badly hurt. A posse turned out with dogs to find the murderers, but to no purpose, although the posse was fired on several times out of ambush. The authorities in that parish seem incapable of making arrests of the perpetrators of these numerous assassinations that occur among them, but when by some chance an arrest is made, no jury is found that will convict. The result is that outlaws have everything their own way, while the peaceable people have no assurance that at any moment they will not be murdered by cowardly assassins."

Thus it is that the southern white people, by permitting a few desperate politicians to outlaw the

Negro, find themselves at the mercy of an oligarchy which has everything its own way.

According to the census of 1890, there are 102,657 white male citizens of voting age in South Carolina and 132,947 colored male citizens of voting age, making a total of 253,604 male citizens who were entitled to vote in that year. The election returns from that state for November 1898 show that the highest total vote polled for any office was only 28,258, averaging less than eight hundred votes to each county, thus showing that less than one eighth of the male citizens have it in their power to control the administration and policies of the state.

If by a mere technicality one class of citizens can be deprived of the rights and immunities guaranteed by the organic law of the nation, what is to prevent any other class from sharing the same fate? If less than one fourth of the male citizens of Mississippi can usurp the right to exclusively manage the local government, what is to prevent a smaller proportion from doing the same? If it is possible for a minority of the people of Alabama to disfranchise one class of citizens on account of race without the consent of the majority, what is to prevent the disfranchisement of any other class on account of political views? Southern white men who view with apprehension these untoward political tendencies, who are alarmed at the passing away of the last vestiges of a republican form of government from that section of our

Union, and who silently condemn and deplore the outrageous and inexcusable manner in which the black man is being divested of his political and civil rights for mere party advantage, must seriously and actively face the situation, if they would save the south from the shame and the humiliation with which she is threatened, and which she has already too keenly experienced at the hands of a profligate leadership.

There is a dormant statesmanship in the south that must and will exert itself mightily, "a moral and intellectual intelligence which is not going to be much longer beguiled out of its moral right of way by questions of political punctilio, but will seek that plane of universal justice and equity which it is every people's duty before God to seek."

But the question is not a sectional one. The whole American people are deeply concerned in it. Nullification in South Carolina is as great a national menace today as it proved to be half a century ago. Republican institutions and the national welfare can have no guarantee or protection against the evil consequences threatened by defiant trampling upon constitutional authority. Not in its most palmy days did the slave system possess such power as is aimed at by these latter day nullifiers. Having shorn the Negro of his political rights and brought him into industrial subjection, thereby usurping power both in state and national government, they now threaten to dominate the economic and industrial policies of the nation.

This government can not long continue half republican in form and half oligarchic.

JOHN L. LOVE.